Future Blues
Michael S. Begnal

salmonpoetry

Published in 2012 by
Salmon Poetry
Cliffs of Moher, County Clare, Ireland
Website: www.salmonpoetry.com
Email: info@salmonpoetry.com

Copyright © Michael S. Begnal, 2012

ISBN 978-1-907056-90-1

All rights reserved. No part of this publication may be reproduced or transmitted in any form or by any means, electronic or mechanical, including photography, recording, or any information storage or retrieval system, without permission in writing from the publisher. The book is sold subject to the condition that it shall not, by way of trade or otherwise, be lent, resold or otherwise circulated without the publisher's prior consent in any form of binding or cover other than that in which it is published and without a similar condition, including this condition, being imposed on the subsequent purchaser.

COVER ARTWORK: *Kyle Fitzpatrick*, "Theater" (mixed media on canvas, 95" x 96", 2007), www.kylefitzpatrick.com
COVER DESIGN: *Siobhán Hutson*

Salmon Poetry receives financial support from The Arts Council

Acknowledgements

Some of the poems in this volume have appeared in the following print and online journals or anthologies:

An Guth, An Sionnach: A Journal of Literature, Culture, and the Arts, Blackbird, The Black Mountain Review, BlazeVOX 2k5 (BlazeVOX Books), *The Blue Canary, Burdock, The Burning Bush 2, Crannóg, Dark Sky, Eyewear, Feasta, The Fifteen Project, FIRE, Free Verse, Go Nuige Seo* (Coiscéim), *GRASP, Honeysuckle, Honeyjuice: A Tribute to James Liddy* (Arlen House), *Iota, Kill Poet, KIOSKO, :lexicon, MungBeing, Natural Bridge, Notre Dame Review, Otoliths, Pense Aqui, PIG: a journal, Pittsburgh Post-Gazette, Poets for Living Waters, Poiesis, Reprint Poetry, Suisun Valley Review, TINGE Magazine, Triskele, Windhover, Winter Tales* (Serving House Books), and *ZYX*.

Thanks to Willie Brown for the title.

Contents

Silver Ghosts	11
Blues for Tomorrow	12
Waterworld	14
The Three Phases	15
Day/ Night/ Dawn	18
Grab the Polaroid	20
Primates	21
Homage to Allen Kirkpatrick	22
In the Stadium	27
Sunrise	28
Mountain	29
The Fluctuations	30
At the Cliff	31
Blood or Fire	32
Solitary Room Freak-Outs	33
Éire, san 18ú Aois	34
Mar Mheiriceánach	35
Lá Bealtaine, thar Sáile	36
Ollamh	37
Homage to James Liddy	38
Application for the Provision of Catholic Beverages	39
Shade	40
Red Horse	42
Bat	44
Dead Rabbits	45

Kells	47
Angles	48
Liberty Cap	49
Bettie Page	50
Homage to Li Po	52
Thylacine	53
Dear _____,	56
Samhain	58
Poem Written in Red Ink on Fluorescent-Yellow Paper	62
Pink Field	63
Dithyramb	64
Horn	65
Line	66
In an Unknown City, It Seemed	67
Station	68
Submerged Town Reappears	69
For Ron Asheton	70
The Stooges' Third Album on Elektra	73
The Red Brick Light	75
Black Dolphins (Palindrome)	76
Tarpit	78
Yellow Wave	79
Manifesto	80
About the Author	85

Silver Ghosts

Silver ghosts gleaming in the meadow
like butterflies
           with razorblade wings
sniffing for pollen
        pink as pure blow—
thereof, and more,
              the poet will sing

Like butterflies with razorblade wings,
slash the clouds into bloody twilight
(thereof, also, the poet must sing),
once again suck the air of black night

Slash the clouds
        into bloody twilight,
celebrate all the dead in their graves,
once again breathe the air of black night—
poems come, furious,
              in light-waves

Celebrate
        all the dead in their graves,
sniffing for pollen pink as pure blow,
poems come, furious, in light-waves:
silver ghosts,
           gleaming in the meadow

Blues for Tomorrow

                                        Gatefold

haven't you always
always stood standing

nobody else will know these,
some vague memory of autonomy
hovering in the daze
so that suddenly
      NOW is called transition

orange and blue
[something scribbled out]
reverberation

future blues/
                        nothing will be okay
                  nothing remains pristine for long
                      stretched out in dark bed,
                    the spectacular lights of death

all this terror,
the flying humanoids in the air for real,
    the sinister people who want
      to come back from the past,
        a leafless time
        that wind shook

standing at the window ledge
looking out at the fields
or on whatever street,
no one feels
       these
           ruins

inside,
in the eyes the flesh and hair
and the hair juts below the belly,
                                            line

                    and even below, the dark of the nest

Waterworld

GLUG-GLUG-GLUG, the rainwater
off the outside of the bldg.,
still voices talking below the open window,

today a film of blue sky remained
behind the swirling dark smoky clouds
which suddenly opened up,
bullets fell in multiple volleys on roof slates,
the cats scurried to their dens in disgust,

with a preponderance of daylight re-emerging
I took to the asphalt,
at the bridge I was engulfed

wedged into the right angle of a
rough stone smithy wall / corrugated metal sheet
a tangled branchy mass of ivy hanging overhead,
I wondered what would happen
if I chewed the leaves

stood and imagined the Belgic invasion,
how they came ashore in boats,
waded among the reeds, the marshes, the rushes,
marched along the esker,
built avenues into Turoe
and established their seat

each death finds me in a new location,
a gigantic puddle in the middle of Shop St.,
soon the winter will come,

      r e i n c a r n a t i o n   back on the agenda

The Three Phases

    1.

She opens what is shut, hips alabaster and soft,
bright flower trembling on a breeze,
petals with the feel of skin/ or
skin smooth like fresh leaves in spring

and the words from her fresh lips
are units of poetry, drops of rain
cascading into kisses wet and flurried,
her verbs secret milk you swallow
so that your eyes are clean and glowing

gile na gile, she lives in the fertile crescent,
maybe you visit her, she may visit you,
at times she go her way alone
carrying an egg through plentiful foliage
until a clearing emerges from the thicket,
there's leeway all around, a sudden warmth,

and as you look with your clean and glowing eyes
upon the pools of her absence, an idea forms,
first as a marble, finally in dialect:
    "If it is really you that write this,
    and I am but a conscious vehicle,
    there comes the question of moral light—"

2.

Who dares goes willingly into the struggle,
ah the struggle, face all flushed,
metal bedposts in a hotel room,
the violence that she would give of herself,
her body rippling, rippling like a sea
below, the oxygen gnashing in the ears

that love brings along bottles tipped over,
exposes in fire action
a record of stains in society,

that the moon hangs red like hair
through an open window, then strews
its ray right across her open mouth,
lips curled up, an expression of liquid assent,
of expansion in your common plane here

down the halls of memory her face blurs
in shadow, every instant a different girl
who abandons in turn to be supplanted
by the next incarnation of view,
in secret rooms no lack of communication,
hours go down like the minutes, until
there is but one image, her glimmering glory: behold

3.

The music was sinister, iterative, and
the crowd's pills didn't work but waned,
you stood uncaged, had souls filling your mouth—
I watched your former selves spectrally
on the stage, the music was sinister and old

cold wind cutting, but no one cared,
not you, *ceann dubh*, who were indifferent
to a shrunken condom in my front pocket,
or the man not unlike me, mute I guess,
who you lured into the lavatory
and poisoned with yew (especially),
and the music pounding terrible and cold,

it was as if I was drowning in that river,
floating back, head tilted under and water seeping in
everywhere, a frog kicking across my nose
—tell my mother it will be okay!—
but it won't you said silently
your black eyes spelling out all,
so that I knew finally of the apples,
would know again the tedium of the familiar/

my songs all of lonesome, she shuts the door

Day/ Night/ Dawn

Distorted reflections in the windshield
of an oncoming bus (coming round a turn)
face looking forward,
walking on freshly-tarred footpaths
into the glass,
caught then my own sudden expression
       in rays

•

at night, floodlights on the clouds like gotham

the way everyone's all suspicious,
in bars the usual eyes down
(now you're definitely out of their situation)
but the beats really on,
always wafting just over the heads of the people
I treaded in, as a sea,
lurking, looking out, taking the sound in,
don't know what record revolving on turntable two
but guys were trading off raps,
putting out some heavy flashes
and there were girls dancing
and in another time I'da felt good

> *when we climbed over the gate and walked out the weir,*
> *jet engine sound of the cold rushing fall below,*
> *drank an open can of beer, some Scotch,*
> *and threw the empty bottle in*

•

the bleak greys of morning,
the sky's volcanoes erupt,
magenta orange smeared on the horizon,

walking towards home I guess, rubber legs,
the sun in all the wrong places
so the river has a sudden clarity,
the colors in the grass,

The Thin Red Line

tis war all the time

Grab the Polaroid

Grab the polaroid
and head down to where they spray graffiti
on brick walls
and piss in alleys

the canal flows nearby
clogged with dead leaves of limitless autumns,
sometimes with suicides—
I mean that wasn't no dream
when you saw the police at the iron railing
looking down

or instead the river's mouth
at high tide a vast black pool,
cormorants wrestle with writhing eels,
      light glints
            on rubbery scales
     iron-blue beak
           swallows alive—

don't drop off the edge of the
                        earth

Primates

His eyes intimate knowledge, this chimpanzee,
sparkling with the iron light of sentience,
we will have to expand our conception of the word
      HUMAN,
he is maybe the poet of his tribe and wizened
leader whom the others in the photo silently acquiesce to,
his mind forms open lines of hairy thought
knitted in his point in time and forest order

I, again, am alone in the mirror,
older now, a delicate cracking around the eyes,
nail-head pupils and my lashes are a mess,
this is not a photo but an instant never reoccurring,
eternal, 3:10 A.M. between golden bathroom walls—
      sapience: unknown—
this face so secretly and fiercely familiar,
I will open another can of beer now but

tomorrow I will kill the poachers
    / I will murder the colonists
    / I will cut down the loggers
    / I will exterminate all the brutes

Homage to Allen Kirkpatrick

*All this in the eye of one who sought
and seeing set it down.*

—CARL CHOSEED, "An Elegy for R. Allen Kirkpatrick"

[1967]

The recording of the observable world

2nd Day Methedrine, a photo:
Lower East Side / b&w / 1967
my uncle in the left foreground,
Allen standing, his then wife (with horn rims),
my mother and father when I was 1,
a black man in the background
leaning against the metal railing with camera around his neck,
background trees in summer leaf and POLICE LINE

the painting of the photo:
now he puts himself behind the lens
colors dripping with come-down clarity,
is it the same scene, paint instead of light absorbed,
the tint of nostalgia, media layered upon each other,
a fungus intervention
        lost juxtaposition   2nd parallel
                  meta-

    images, no longer static

[1972]

Orange Jesuit:
    ex-cathedra
  setting sun on the rooftops
hazy evening on the river
    docks bathed in orange
  smokestacks & steeples
light glinting on water   windows
    the water-tanks in relief
      triangular light
        reflections

"orange juice is good and good *for* you"
dream images transposed to celluloid
leafy shadows waving through your head
the filmmaker lies in black repose
    drink-sick

Krishnas dancing on concrete Manhattan streets/
Catholic priests,
    they just stand around smoking cigarettes,
    druidical Irish faces with sideburns

      the (suspension) bridge

stained glass rose window round / film reel spinning

      dead dog decaying in the gutter/
heart rears wings

    out among the trees
      ultra-montane
        joy

[1973]

Naples and I Must Supply the World with Noodles:
rabbit ears TV-set close up on screen,
Pepsi Generation broken bottle knife fight
Black Panther molotov cocktails
glass dildo suicide pills commercial

the cavalcade of official limousines,
dignitaries at the inauguration

    the lone sniper, his rifle held aloft,
    in black the grim reaper of the rooftop
        shoots,
    white chalk on the door: "NAPLES AND I…"
    the getaway assassin down flights of stairs

mannequins in windows, lone wanderings,
Times Sq. neons of 42nd St. porno moviehouses,
rainy reflections on the slick pavements
    the inverted skyline
down at the demonstration amid Vietcong banners,
the red star, cameras clicking everywhere the news

Nixon on TV / swallow a razorblade

    gun-toting narcissus revolutionary chic
    flashing lights naked in the mirror
    the mirror within the mirror
    the light hits your face is red, Red, RED!

To be Revolutionary/
the True Revolutionary seeks new forms,
we must have new images and modes of being

an Asian wearing headphones &
listening to bugging equipment in your spare room

holding a knife his eyes pierce red your paranoia,
   look again: the room is empty
      and again: TV-set, rabbit ears

         the lone assassin his rifle held ready
         in black the shadow on the rooftop
            shoots,

      on TV, white chalk: "NAPLES AND I…"

   [1975]

Adrenalin Devours the Blood:
the filmmaker holds up (again) the mirror to himself
reads yesterday's paper
and the news may not be good
(a drinking contest left two friends dead),
      Manhattan approached
         with dread along the surface of the river

Kill Yr Sons/
Lou Reed iconic footage his poetry, gestures,
jerking motions like the the sound is dis-juncted,
a hand-held camera observes
gay pride parade black balloon leather boys
cops guns and the American flag,
boxing bout KO in the ring
and sleeping bums head on curb
under the belly of New York
secret filming of junkyards

O sadness of
first-thing-in-the-morning bars
old men's whiskey and water shot glasses
dolorous light through translucent curtains,
bathroom urinals—

silhouetted against the color cathode test signal
the filmmaker examines strips of his film,
x-rays of the salacious/
      the blind beggar solicits change

the black hooker beautiful mounds of flesh
to strains of "Angel Baby" breasts hang
projected in shadow then lumined and brown
"it's just like heaven, being here with you"
Allen visible in the hotel room mirror
just as I am visible in the writing of the poem
combs her hair in the mirror angel baby
as he films holding camera 16mm,
yes let us see the mechanics,
"ooh-hoo I love you" coarse black pubic hair

graffiti subway train cars
running up the screen 3-D style
SCAT   CODE   THE DR. J JET CHEF FAT
have got up too in spray-paint

the transsexual classic American
70s housewife style heavy eye makeup & hair

(Allen again visible in the mirror,
      a heavy hand)
street scene pimps, wigs in shop windows
XXX cinema Playmate Studio 25¢ booths
      vicious
O sweet Lou in double exposure
light glints on guitar like flickering neon
gay parade glamour queen floats of America,

      and the universe

In the Stadium

the stadium of white stone,
cracked blocks of sun

        faces brown and lined,
the men eating tacos in the stands,
some take pills when no one is looking

hard working in the taxi office 12 hours a day,
it's hard sitting in these faulty seats of wood
which date to Roman times or before,
and the peanut vendors never come around

    it is that
the colossal stadium
        has gathered the people—

the announcer, drunk, crackles over the loudspeaker,
you peer through an arch on the mezzanine
and view its space/

    the stadium at night,
        floodlights shoot into the black sky,
            cathedral columns spaced in circle
so when you look up, the whole crowd one mass,
        as in its womb,
            enwrapped in its familial warmth,
you see a passage, or a canal,

    you rise through it,

        up,
        up,
        up,

      to birth

Sunrise

Pink and mottled through the clouds,
    an old man
    carrying a satchel,
he is queer,
and he speaks Chinese

Mountain

the sky strangely shimmering,
the town revealed from it
misplaced with distance, its
plan of streets indiscernible to the retina's rods
       and cones,

instead more mountains on the blue horizon,
seriate ridges stretching out in parallel,

and we inhabit merely one of numerous valleys

       and somewhere underneath,
       say 1′ down,
       arrowheads,
       fang of a mountain lion,

              a clearing
                of

The Fluctuations

THE FLUCTUATIONS are real,
they warp you sere & black,
they sear you from the inside,
that part of the body

the FLUCTUATIONS,
a transmigration of soul,
lost genealogies, rocky estuary, the Iron Language,
rain, a structuring gloom—GONE

the fluctuations/
(running through the trenches)
a torrent in a dark room, breath pouring through,
alone in the room don't know how again

(it's the fluctuations)
the zephyrs in the night,
the curtains blowing in somebody else's window,
the charry dry alleys

death & loss dripping from your eyes,
death & loss seeping from your lungs,
death & loss in your twisted black guts like shit,
in the stark stochastic scald

At the Cliff

Warm at the cliff,
the air swollen moist like after rain,

time wilts and willows,
residue builds sweet on the tongue,

and the fireflies light up the night
in swarms

Blood or Fire

And the people were all against you,
at least as much as when you were a foreigner,
the importance of experience
of suffering together in a dark basement

and the way they were set against each other,
what a sad thing to call home,
a thousand cuts,
like broken beer bottles on a concrete floor:
fear stalks "the scene"

the double-o, half-glimpsed faces encircled you,
projected back a history you could not recognize,
the shock of that,
how it was different from the expectation,
as a stylized "big lie" delivered
in a certain locality's impenetrable dialect,
the distance to anyone next table,
a balkanization, almost political

> the season turned deranged,
> the animals antagonized in their ditches,
>
> tree leaves bright-reddened and fell:
> blood or fire,
>
> the mountain ridges were *walls* of fire
> but at night were dark as clouds

Solitary Room Freak-Outs

Solitary room freak-outs nobody knows the panic of white paint has no country,

outside, the tree roots peed on, fingers wiped on bark,

I have been here before

Éire, san 18ú Aois

Faoi cheobhrán an Tí Mhóir
ritheann na capaill deargrua amach
i dtreo na gcoillte ngearrtha,

roinnt cruamhíle ó shin
tá bothán dubh ar an sliabh
ina bhfuil fear féasógach,

le geamhsholas an tinteáin,
déanann sé stáidéar ar leabhair
(ní fhaigheann sé mórán ach fionna),

sroicheann capall aonair an bun,
dreapann sé suas, suas, suas, agus
buaileann ar an doras le crúb—

"Tar isteach...?"

Mar Mheiriceánach

Garbh doilbh liom an Ghaeilge oscailte—is olc an comhartha é.
—Pádraig Ó Héigeartaigh, "Ochón! a Dhonncha"

Mar a scaipeamar ariamh
bhíomar scaipthe trasna na bóchna glaise
de bharr ocrais, a dúradh, an t-am sin,
nó mar gheall ar thoradh an ocrais,
más féidir a rá go dtáinig rud éicínt as anrud

—ar fhás crann ariamh as cac?—

agus sinn gortaithe, thuirling
ar bhruach aisteach coincréite
mar Indiaigh dhúchasacha ag filleadh ón mbás,
treabhach, ag éirí ón sáile
gan ach cúpla focal Béarla "sa bhád uilig"

agus d'eagraíomar sinn féin
i measc na gcaolsráideanna, na mblocanna,
mar a d'eagraigh ariamh

ag lorg oibre,

agus bhrúigh siad a bpian isteach
sna seanmóirí eaglaise a bhí ag callaireacht i gcoinne *abolition*,
sna piléir a pholl craiceann dearg na ndúchasach ar na mánna,
sna smachtíní péas a chnag cloigne gorma ó am go chéile,
sa lámh fhionn a ghreamaigh gloine i gcúinne dorcha an bheáir
i gcúl tí ag taibhriú ar thráthanna níos fearr

Lá Bealtaine, thar Sáile

B'fhearr na rainn a chumadh
agus tuirse ort, easpa suain
nó go dtiocfadh aislingí sa dhúiseacht,
nó, mar a déanadh roimh éag do Mhongán,
riamh i seomra dorcha
ag déanamh aithrise ar chodladh aríst
nach dtagann—

cuardaíonn tú leabhar nótaí,
láithríonn buidéal beora,
teilifíseán ar *MUTE*,

cat i bhfuinneog trasna na sráide
ag breathnú ort
trí theas tiubh an tráthnóna—

    tine   *tine*

Ollamh

Nuair a bhíos níos óige
b'é an séasúr is fearr

ná an samhradh, ach
i mbliana is é an t-earrach:

an méid sin peiteal
ar na bláthanna,

an méid sin bláthanna
ar na crainn,

an méid sin cleití
ar mo thuighean,

agus mise i m'ollamh

Homage to James Liddy

It might be that Ireland is an illusion,
> Brasil,
disappearing into western sea haze
> beyond Aran

it might be that America is abstract,
> doesn't exist,
falling in the mind a decadent city
> beyond Aran,

yet somewhere someone foots a lane,
a tangible cobble / someone
stands on the corner of the boulevard,

and we give them our respect,
because we are not so fortunate
> to be poets

Application for the Provision of Catholic Beverages

The priest wipes down the bar with a moldy cloth,
spirits pour into a glass,
leans back in black shirt-sleeves,
some customer (placed his money
on the damp finish of wood)
gulps the shot, bangs the glass down

deeper in along the bar,
dim but for the lamp above,
    and behind the bottles and stacks of glasses
    the mirror

the front door opens to admit another patron,
a hinting gust of outside air seeps in,
the door clatters closed,
    low sounds of a muffled order
        then a dusty silence

at closing the priest pours a shot for himself,
then a second, his stiffened white collar loosens,
white hair falls out of place, he
lights a cigarette butt,

sits alone behind the bar, does not invoke words,
waits for the customers to finish and leave
(per terms of the liquor license),

a silent recognition: "We have stopped serving"

Shade

/BLACK LODGE/
or like Joyce in Skerries

has gone back to dark his hair and beard
but he is somewhat out of it,
does not speak much at all often,
SIBYLLINE his few words and sentences

or sick and dying pretends health
in a black turtleneck, can of Schaefer,
tossing the can away leaning against my shoulder,
"I've been drinking all week,

    it's the only way I feel good"

or like really the first time the lodge
appeared as the living room of house
and there was a vision of the Cross
in cathode light behind my eyelids

spoke of secret children, other chambers,
information he had wanted to impart and
yet which was also corrupt—I wondered
what way was Persephone's land

    from which no man returns,

heaven or hell or wherever
or my grandmother's old kitchen
in cinder-block public housing,
was cooking a big bunch of bacon (he

spread "jalapeño butter" on first
["It cultures it"], before the frying pan)—
to stand in the kitchen, and to know of women:
"Your whole mood depends on the economy"

    he liked when I said that,

I gave him an old newspaper in the room,
we went downstairs, the little child was with us
like the dream where the child smiles and says hello,
it was as if it was there all along

but in the carriage weak and frail, and that
"the streets look like they're having sex"
—I put my arm around him—
I knew he was not a hole in the ground

Red Horse

Galloping on lone leg outside of your window,
the racket brings you out

      a copse,
            a vast room,

                sparsely treed
and enclosed by a ceiling of darkness,

an capall dearg
turns then and looks at your eyes,

onto the flat plain, panged
you fall to the ground

        •

El Camino de la Muerte

after you went off the cliff,
after you fell for a minute,
shaken in a van through the air

after you lay strewn blue and rotten
and peasants looted your belongings
in which amid broken wrenched bodies/

where is the central government?
apparently there are really llamas,
a leaféd jungle aspect

branches along which insects have walked,
that have shot up from dirt and clay
along the overgrown faces

a hundred years ago a llama fetus
withered brown in the sun, stenched,
and the slow goo of ants, a nearby river

a flying insect several feet in daylight above
silently feels the best at what it does:
unfortunate, will be snuffed

•

drifting through the arcade,
the Dickhouse bar upstairs,

on the couch sitting
in the dark light

distant, didn't really want to
at first talk to them,

said she was bored there,
bored,

some formula of gravity
it's all too much/

k e e p   i n

t o u c h

Bat

The five mammalian fingers,

      the

          five

          bone

          mammalian

          fingers/

furry little animal
quivering by the ceiling,

a wing
and a claw,
        come
        through a wall:

lit space, terror,

      chirps

          at   e v o l v e d   frequencies,

            in terror

Dead Rabbits

plastic

mouths stained green with chlorophyll,
the corpses lined the roadside then

the economy warped in its spasms,
died or passed to America—

the books and documentaries show
that they too faced racists,
spit, hierarchies of birth/
organized, meshed,
replicated themselves
in new city scenes (new sods)

yet it all came down to cocaine,
the Italians?

software technology after midnight,
and shamrock is just clover?

paddy

•

far from the gateway cities,
in the blanched blended town
(once a muddy trading post),
clean schools, polluted creek

old ladies in lawn chairs
lining the street on the 4th of July
pelted with candy by nubile
cheerleaders from platform trucks/

the house made of stone and wood
contained a Book: *The Táin*
(trans. Kinsella), text in b/w (/red),
brush of le Brocquy, streaked, ink spatters

the father on a drunk summer night
(warm enough for bikini underwear)
with his friend throwing rocks
at the streetlight swarming with insects

Kells

There was land somehow, but not enough,
a mist on the Galway-to-Dublin road

like something out of Twilight verse,
then darkness passing Milltownpass, so

a shot of whiskey for Muiris [†1528], transcriber
of texts medical and, let us say, otherwise,

"with Unction and Penance"
a shot for Donnchadh too, his father,

like something out of *Ancestor Worship*,
dark and not enough,

and Conaing Ua Beiccleiġinn [†1128]
"Abbot of Ceanannus, died"—

Ceanannus is Kells, so a shot for Conaing, who
kept custody of the Book in the candled sacristy

ruined, and a grassy green,
intimations of gold (whiskey as medicine)

covered in mist, and somewhere further beyond,
the first of the name, a scholar

covered too in medicine,
in intimations of gold

Angles

The Angles are coming!
keels on the shore,

forays across the sea in keels,
heaved oars, hacked the sea,

forced the WEALES west again,
a planting of language,

the ground cultivated,
a displacement of DNA,

sex in the swamps as advertised in print,
drunken soldiers looking for a plantation

the rustling grasses breezily cut,
the insecure gardens of violence,

trimmed bushes regimented in rows,
as Malick put it,

trade winds dance,
agrarian economy, multiple-harvest,

the difference between
the forest vs. the goods,

a yield of such commodities,
such commodities,

more, more,
        more, more, more

Liberty Cap

purge through fear,
a reign of terror,
revolution

stricken and disgusted by words,
a hard place and a rock,
fires (coming fire)

then a slow walk through town
where the moon is overrun
with drifts of snow
and waits up the path

and on the frame of the picture
fungus figures dancing,
like saying hello

a metaphor:
they're wearing "liberty caps"

Bettie Page

> *"I had less sex activity those seven years in New York than I had any other time in my life."*

She is always in a room,
which may be a dwelling of the dead
or the isolated cum-house of deviants

or rather, an apartment
with a disconnected telephone
where she is lured and tied
    to a chair
    with ropes

black her hair
and pale white skin,
the classic black/white,
"raven" "porcelain"

her black bangs
which would later be emulated
by hip strippers in their pinup crazes,
who aspired to appear in *Vue*,
    the pinup craze

everyone wanted to date her
(she radiated blackly)
"Can I date you?" "Yes..."
so she dated them and men dated her,
and they sat on benches in parks
and dated

at beaches also she became unclothed,
but it was better in rooms
/always I refuse to be dead/

she said and took off her clothes
when the camera was alone

her skirt off and dresses and blouses
showing her underwear and mouth,
she was dating,
she could be very dark
   ~~sexless~~
     and

   so,

when from the mouth it radiates
and her eyes wonder who it is that's watching,
when the tattered newsprint pages of *Chicks and Chuckles*
are blown down the winter alleyway
and clay collects in the cracks below the window
and the furniture begins to show its age—

Bettie Page,

    Bettie Page,

        Bettie Page

Homage to Li Po

The leaves turn in the October sun,
top of a tree the color of wine,

its lower leaves still clinging to green—
useless, they too will soon curl and fall,

to be whirled away in the cold wind
and decay in the grass, so I sit,

open my bottle of Taylor Port,
which will be empty before sunset

Thylacine

With a loping run across a road
he disappears again into trees,

the loneliness must be much more
than just a drag,

like the time I woke up in a dream
in this couple's apartment,

didn't know them at all
and had to leave immediately,

but their stuffed thylacine
came alive and smiled,

his eyes glowed then and
seemed almost to speak

•

on black-and-white film
he paces a cage,

why should I be tortured like this?
antagonized and confined,

stripes evolved for grasses, bush,
not bars or chicken-wire,

the difference between a 'solitary nature'
and involuntary seclusion—

to be denied the camaraderie
of fellow furréd beings—

I am forced into this room,
through the door, her insoluble angers

•

or, stripes evolved
for individual recognition/

the smile of his happy jaws
crushed out

yeah that's right—
 fuck you imperialism
  or whatever,
  just fuck you
and never again trouble us
 or our pouched species

fuck you and your northern
hemisphere reference points,
 of "hyaena" or "wolf" or "tiger"—
  you don't understand our point of view

you leave our carcasses to rot,
you bring yourselves bad weather

•

don't you understand, nobody
has ever acted like this toward me

before,
and it is really freaking me out/

a marsupial face
emerges from the tree line

edged in sun
on the beach,

another one
exits behind rocks, and

they will never see each other
again

Dear _____,

Just to let you know
I finally got the window open,
now all these screams come in
and red air
bearing dragonflies,

when I said before, "It ain't summer
if you can't lie awake at night
with the windows open,"
I must've been living in a cold climate,

you'd think I had icebergs in my veins

fact now I'm pretty melted,
it's all solar tears
shining from my eyes,
a blinding white wall—

the longer time goes on
the stranger the memories,
a cat waking from a dream
in a darkened room

        one has me on Banba's shore
inside a drizzly pub,
a small hit of hash
through a clay pipe

the rough coast

an empty apartment
viewed through a partly opened door,

you know, I can't help thinking
it's like it all never existed,
and now you're getting translucent—
will you too really fade?

        Love,

Samhain

> *The figure of Mongán deserves particular attention since he plays a major role in certain compositions which have the whiff of paganism to them.... Mongán was a 7th-century chief who remained sympathetic to pagan thinking...and the poets looked to him as a leader and source of hope as they attempted to stand against Christianity.*
>
> —WILLIAMS & NÍ MHUIRÍOSA, *Traidisiún Liteartha na nGael*, 1979 [trans. MSB]

for Mongán

for all the dead who have spoke before
me   spoke for all the dead who have before
spoke   for all the dead who have before
dead   for all who have spoke before the
me

I trust in language always

a world without ownership

get in all of it,
       it leads to where
         there is

a flicker in an empty room of light
not your own

an amp loud with reverb

a poets' rebellion
ancient revolutionary movement
forever,

the ground's flesh,

where do you end?

>for all the dead
>spoke for
>spoke for all
>dead for all
>me

I trust in a world, in a flicker,
in a echo,
speak, and they are present,
the words have already
been breathed out their mouths,
and tongued

they are there, in a word or line
you thought was your own,
and walk among us to
>night

•

>*dosnig am-muír fri tír toind,*
>*trilsi glano asa moing*
>>—Imram Brain maic Febail

>*the sea washes a wave against land,*
>*hair of crystal from its mane*
>>—The Voyage of Bran

quiet and sweet silver
he was bright

the sea's mane,
militant foam
monged

sweet militant,
start gathering words/

>   amp forever loud
>   with ancient rebellion,
>   flesh movement,
>   the amber liquid ours,
>   we suck each other's breasts

sun going down on the sea
and we are still wet,
warm

a hand moves to music,
"my hair is a sea-blue"

sea silver / son of the sea
on a kind of land

there are numerous languages,
fading light

•

amp loud with reverb
air moves through
as a wind

breathed out the mouth and
through you, re/
          spire

electric amp forever
loud with re/
          verb

speak/ again
they are present,
in a echo

all the dead
    moving on the wind
        through you

all the dead
    going down on the sea
        through you

all the dead
    on a kind of land
        through you

all the dead
    gathering words
        through you

all the dead
silver and loud
on the wind

blowing through you,
waves of sea
washing against the land,

the wind rushing in waves
roaring loud
shakes leaves from the

    branch

Poem Written in Red Ink on Fluorescent-Yellow Paper

Walls of red brick looming above,
vents & black metal railings &
industrial air-conditioning fans
spinning to blindness,
streaks of rust drip down the concrete,
        twenty feet,

sun beats bright on the
    NO PARKING
      ANY
      TIME
      ↔
      sign

    half in shade, a tree
      tangled in the shadows of its branches,
     roots underneath the tarmac,

piles of pallets
& another broad wall of brick—

     a delivery truck drives in

Pink Field

Pink glows
off the trees
in the morning cool,

in the pink field

picking

        flower

Dithyramb

The more things change
the more they change, they change:

immortal impossible but
to live long enough

to revolve in the woods, a clearing,
eyes burning with pollen,

the birds enplumed in their trees
will fledge, one after another

night of cars' bass vibrating, dopplerizing,
sirens screaming, fading,

a black cat there certainly crouching
under a bush/

    then I enter the poem,
    and am immediately strong-armed
    into a dark garage
    where there are no shining mirrors,
    no strains of deathless song,
    and leering toughs make gestures
    hierarchical and lost,

    they claim they can define
    everyone, that I'm this or a that,
    a maker of cloudy cadence, couth—
    but of course it's bullshit

        and I'm out along the leaves,
        olive-green under the
        streetlight lampglow,
        the leaves, wet and slick
        and always

            moving

Horn

Called a horn

'cause it's an animal's horn,
an animal of the forest,
or the field

the sound is
weird as an animal
when man is
disaffected from the forest
as she so obviously is

I like it weird,
I like to feel weird
in the house that I rent
and think of the forest
and the fields—

    someday I will go
        to the grove

Line

The smell of sulphur on a hot June night,
a double-bottle of Taylor Port calimocho,
condensation over the glass
of the glass,
and the cat's down in the gutter,

there really is a train whistle out there,
and I could follow the tracks
through strange southern towns,
down tree-stump streets
with badly-sprayed graffiti,

jacket collar getting greasy,
the cuffs frayed,
too hot anyway,
wanna follow that 'Sur 13'
all the way to Spain

                ―――
                there
                is always
                    a line

In an Unknown City, It Seemed

(Like a story after wine)

in this part of the city
were buildings
when you looked at them closer
were constructed of Mayan ruins,

the older Mayan structures reused
and built into,

why I hadn't noticed quite before—

I saw him then, in amongst the buildings,
enclosed in a fenced area,
with a swing-set

I said, these buildings were made of Mayan ruins
but I don't know if you can see
from your vantage point,

went in there to him,
the wire obscured the view yes
but I saw he could see,

told me something
that I could not translate
to the world,

I went into the building that was behind us,
asked to speak to the head of the order,
and a man came out of a door
like a priest
to see me

Station

As ever in the grey concrete
his image blue and

was pixelated,
at the station looked back

or whatever,
concrete, he said

he was going to catch a train
and I left

when I was run-down
they thought

    for city sidewalks

Submerged Town Reappears

It reappears intact
if a little rotten,
some muted green
turning to moss,

its little houses
dark and brown, and
through one window
a drowned bush—

what rows I could have
in the swampy streets,
what seeds would hatch
of wrack and pain

and loss

For Ron Asheton

volume

      volume   volume

  volume

       volume

  the

volume   volume   volume

    volume,

        no way,

chord   chord   chord

    chord

        chord   chord
chord

    chord

        chord

  one two three four,
  thousand—

we mythologize and love our heroes
and propagate their images,

quantum leaps of evolution,
it is nothing else but
and
    and
  and
      and
             and

and the thing
you don't understand at first
is best
    (like a toupée)

something is a part of someone,
never a dead end,
never hard to understand

a bloody hand

    and

―――

(volume)

the shifting sands

what are the sensations
in the studio
under pink,
  looking
for a place called Stoogeland?

other times alone
and drinking,
a mind wide enough
as liquid,
  a switch—

can't ask him now
of the sensation,
songs of a single chord,
quite other song,
the true sound of metal guitar strings
struck through loud
amplifiers,

a strange orange wind wails,
a strange orange wind wails,
    now
an orange wind wails,

        wails

            it wails—

        it's 2009

The Stooges' Third Album on Elektra

Recorded 1971,
has got to be called *I Got a Right*, right?

Side One
   1. I Got a Right (3:57)
   2. You Don't Want My Name (5:13)
   3. Fresh Rag (4:38)
   4. Dead Body (7:01)

Side Two
   1. Big Time Bum (6:11)
   2. Do You Want My Love? (12:27)

Produced by Don Gallucci

the cover, generally speaking,
has a blue motif (in contrast
with the orange of *Fun House*)

it's possible that some of the songs
had different titles and some of the lyrics
evolve in the studio in recording—

on the album, with a degree of separation,
James Williamson's guitar playing
is just as prominent as Ron Asheton's,
and Jimmy Recca's bass too
is heavily recorded—

recorded in the late summer of 1971
and released in early '72,
I Got a Right did not chart,
it was a gimmick they said,
what they always say,
            yeah...

then later it became
a Rhino Handmade re-release
with complete sessions and outtakes,
a three-disc set with extensive
liner notes,

    and I wrote them

The Red Brick Light

Red brick light
projected
onto the apartment wall,
    eight minutes aglow,
about as long as the Stooges song
"Head On"

Black Dolphins

The ocean, rain
lightly drops onto waves,

a dolphin in the moving
surface of the sea,

black back
and a fin

pan across the water
breathing, he breathes, and

a low dune,
a can of beer,

little crests coming in
sideways etc.,

their light captured somewhere,
dissolving, and out where once

the doldrums stranded
ships on the way to

crests of foam
each unalike as

animals swimming in the
sea-dark sea

•

in the sea-dark dark
swim these mammals,

each an individual person
under sea foam,

ships way out on
the latitudes of time

dissolve,
their light captured somewhere,

and then coming at an angle
a big wave smacks you

swimming drunk,
the warm dunes back there,

breathe, only breathe,
suck air above the water

and finally
the black is back

along the surface of the sea,
black dolphins gliding

then dropping beneath waves
of ocean and rain

Tarpit

Oakwood Cemetery,
Raleigh, N.C.

Underneath lies
the unknown, the underground soldier,
goo, a grave, an ossifer,

the cause ossified, as in life,
in death a drooping flag,
all the decayed penises

become goo,
then someone's memory,
then no one's, not a single bone

and when they say that
the war has "stolen their cocks,"
they mean they dead, underneath,

and if someone could say
"he was related to" or
"strange stars glimmer on us"

would anyone here say
yes, this was another country?
in the War of Man's Aggression,

would anyone say
there was anything left here
but bubbling tar?

Yellow Wave

Yellow ocean wave
cresting at the sand, cresting
toward the reeds in mid-
crest, yellow and speckled with
dark globules, thick black spheres of

pretty yellow sea,
out of whom come bottlenose
baby corpses, the
brown pelican angry and
slick, the hard shell of a sea

turtle spray-painted
with a neon X, you are
X-ed, turtle, you are
X-ed, as if in Walton Ford,
the turtle's death scene, painted,

the pelican, its
hissing ire, an array
of smaller brown birds
beheaded and spirited
away by figures in white

paid to suppress these
images will not seep out,
will not seep out these
secret disposals—but there
is a photo of yellow

wave cresting, splattered
with inkspots running to red
where the light shines through

Manifesto

WHEREAS
they want to kill us—
even now when I stand
with my back to the window
it's like I might get shot
through the blinds—

kill us for our resistance to certain fixities,
    for our opposition to our destruction,
    for death is stasis
        and that poetry moves everywhere,
    for the market reduces to homogeneity
        which also equates to death,
    for the assertion that the poet too
        must be able to make a living,
    for our refusal to fix ourselves
        in time or ink,
    for the ways leopard-like we stand,
        sinews and eyes,
because we will fight
    for the next three thousand years
    as the last three thousand

1/
the poet is a part of the people,
among the most oppressed of people
to ever sprawl on the immanent plain

of grass, instigates through movement
a vision of what (the) people can be
    —if me, why not you?—

different but together and equal,
agency and valency,
multi- Multi- MULTI-

the poem is an action among
the most human (and animal) of actions,
like going into a wood,

as the drum sound on *Fun House*,
the syntax of those beats
recorded on magnetic tape,

as a glade of action, the poem is
momentarily a hovering hummingbird
drinking of our sweet flowers

poetry, whose flag is black and green
and might one day be a field
of red, whose party is ongoing—

we are sympathetic beings,
everyone in those houses
with the glass-brick windows

2/
no "mastery"
nor of language,
but always drifting

and drifting down its streams,
a deep-stream guerrilla
moving his/her body together

on the muddy mossy banks
on a midsummer day,
both in the forest

or the city's indescribable alleys:
masked figures there make
such strange muses,

strange new movements
to come, whensoever and
wheresoever, future or now,

a poetic of liberation,
poems that are not like prose,
poetry has no province

but sometimes a city block aloaf
in summer leaf and ancient neon,
the back yards speckled with clover,

rough poems full of mistakes,
let narrative juxtapositions be
but a metaphor of growth

and ever more fluctuations
wreak their rhythm
on the line—

as in life,
wreak their rhythm
on the line

   3/
but there may be no remedy
for our oppression inasmuch
as it is also all our common death,

in that death is the final oppression,
let us say that it will simply happen
and that I will try to be sincere—

as Ó Rathaille ("cabhair ní ghairfead"),
yet also he is freaking out
("'s mé ag caoi ar bhóithre")

but he cannot know death, who can,
except there is nothing more concrete
than it, nothing more concrete, which

we approach through nude symbols
or images of the dead heroes we love,
and we do love them

and love ourselves like lynxes
bounding down from the wintry copse,
down ridges and

    down through the eras of change:

   life = change
and death is a corpse in the snow

Photograph: Emily Rutter

MICHAEL S. BEGNAL was born in 1966. His previous collections are *Ancestor Worship* (Salmon Poetry, 2007), *Mercury, the Dime* (Six Gallery Press, 2005), and *The Lakes of Coma* (Six Gallery Press, 2003). His poems, essays and reviews have appeared internationally in numerous journals and anthologies, in print and electronically. He was editor of the Galway, Ireland-based literary magazine *The Burning Bush* as well as the book *Honeysuckle, Honeyjuice: A Tribute to James Liddy* (Arlen House, 2006). In 2008, Begnal earned an MFA from North Carolina State University. He currently lives in the city of Pittsburgh where he teaches poetry and composition.

www.mikebegnal.blogspot.com